The material between these covers is derived from varied sources.
Some of the items might technically be termed nursery - rhymes,
however, the nursery in question is more likely to be the open street,
or possibly a room frequented by the family - at - large, rather than
some closeted chamber designed for children to develop, occasionally
seen, but seldom heard.

I have described the collection as having been ' gathered ' in Ireland,
which is true, for such is the case. Yet I would make no claim as to its
being exclusively Irish. The language of children has a communicative
dimension which would make nonsense of such a boast.

Some of the pieces undoubtedly originated in adult surroundings,
in particular the odd snatch of song. These are included because I
heard them actually ' taken-over ' by the children, or indeed adapted
by them to suit their own purposes. Should the adult world register
mild shock at the inclusion of some of the items, I would suggest
that children reflect all facets of life through their own creative play.
It is life as *they* view it, not excluding aspects from which adults
might seek to isolate them.

I am personally grateful to all those — including parents, grandparents
and playmates — who passed on so much of this material to me when
I was a child. Since attaining adulthood many children have added to
this store and to them too I am thankful. In addition I must
acknowledge the insight I have gained from those who have
undertaken special studies of the lore of childhood. In particular I
would commend the work, in various media, of David Hammond,
Brendan Colgan, Eilis Brady and of course Iona and Peter Opie.

In conclusion I must admit to having taken liberties, in the sense that
I am myself responsible for some of these lines. In self - justification I
might claim that I have been sufficiently flattered to have witnessed
these efforts actively accepted by those for whom they were intended.

Bill Meek

This collection is in memory of Bessie, who passed on to me so much of the material. It is also dedicated to children everywhere and in particular my own brood : that is, Eoin, Colm, Sarah and Caitriona — who have now moved on to older things but will remember much of the contents — Paili and Agaigeal — who keep me up to date with more recent versions — and little Laoise — who arrived just in time for the completion of the first draft.

V

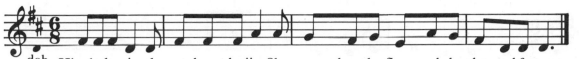

doh Higgledy pig, the cat danced a jig, She pranced on the floor and she shouted for more.

Higgledy pig ,
The cat danced a jig ,
She pranced on the floor
And she shouted for more .

' John come sell your fiddle, if ever you mean to thrive.'
' No I'll not sell my fiddle, to any man alive.
If I should sell my fiddle, the people would think me mad,
For many's the joyful times, my fiddle and I have had.'
' Ah John come sell your fiddle, and buy your wife a gown.'
' No I'll not sell my fiddle, for all of the wives in town.'

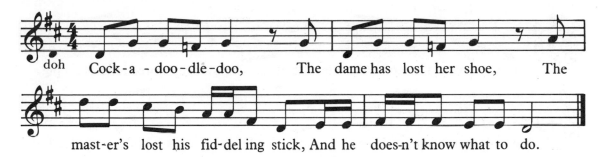

doh Cock-a - doo-dle-doo, The dame has lost her shoe, The mast-er's lost his fid-del ing stick, And he does-n't know what to do.

Cock-a-doodle doo,
The dame has lost her shoe,
The master's lost his fiddling stick
And he doesn't know what to do.

Cock-a-doodle doo,
What is the dame to do ?
Till master finds his fiddling stick
She'll dance without her shoe.

The cat went a-sleep by the side of the fire, The wo-man snored loud as a pig,

Joe took his whist-le at Jin-ny's de-sire, And he struck up a bit of a jig. Jig,Jig!

The cat went asleep by the side of the fire,
The woman snored loud as a pig,
Joe took his whistle at Jinny's desire,
And he struck up a bit of a jig , jig, jig !

THE THREE— HA' PENNY PIG

I   went to the fair at Dun-gan-non,— And bought a three-ha'-pen-ny pig.— I

car-ried it home in my   a-pron,— While dan-cing   a swag-ger-ing   Jig.'—

I went to the fair at Dungannon
And bought a three-ha'penny pig
I carried it home in my apron
While dancing a swaggering Jig .

CHARLIE CHAPLIN

Charlie Chaplin went to France
To teach the ladies how to dance,
Heel to heel and toe to toe,
And all round the G. P. O.

doh Dance thumb-kin dance, Dance thumb-kin dance, Dance you mer-ry men

ev'-ry one, Thumb-kin he can dance a-lone, Dance thumb-kin dance.

Dance Thumbkin dance,
Dance Thumbkin dance,
Dance you merrymen every one,
Thumbkin he can dance alone,
Dance Thumbkin dance.

Dance Pointer dance,
Dance Pointer dance,
Dance you merrymen every one,
Pointer he can dance alone,
Dance Pointer dance.

Dance Middleman dance,
Dance Middleman dance,
Dance you merrymen every one,
Middleman he can dance alone,
Dance Middleman dance.

Dance Ringman dance,
Dance Ringman dance,
Dance you merrymen every one,
Ringman he can dance alone,
Dance Ringman dance.

Dance Littleman dance,
Dance Littleman dance,
Dance you merrymen every one,
Littleman he can dance alone,
Dance Littleman dance.

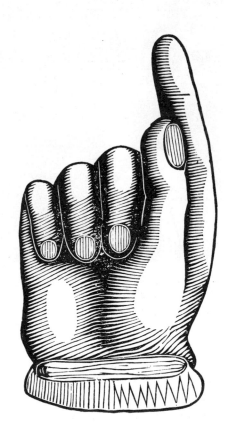

DANCE TO YOUR DADDY

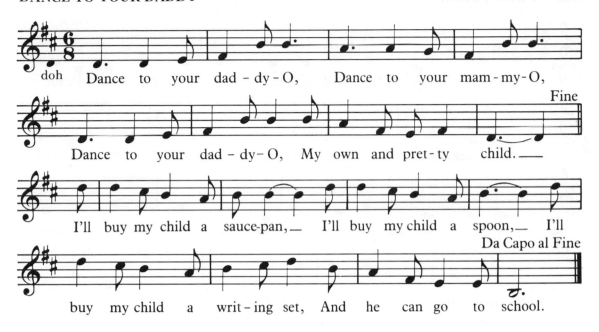

doh Dance to your dad-dy-O, Dance to your mam-my-O,

Fine

Dance to your dad-dy-O, My own and pret-ty child. ___

I'll buy my child a sauce-pan, ___ I'll buy my child a spoon, ___ I'll

Da Capo al Fine

buy my child a writ-ing set, And he can go to school.

Dance to your daddy - o,
Dance to your mammy - o,
Dance to your daddy - o,
My own and pretty child.

I'll buy my child a saucepan,
I'll buy my child a spoon,
I'll buy my child a writing set,
And he can go to school.

Dance to your daddy - o,
Dance to your mammy - o,
Dance to your daddy - o,
My own and pretty child.

WHEN I WAS YOUNG

doh When I was young and had no sense, I bought a fid – dle for eight-een pence, But the on – ly tune that I could play was 'O-ver the hills and far a - way', So ear-ly in the morn-ing, So ear-ly in the morn-ing, So ear-ly in the morn-ing, Be – fore the break of day.

When I was young and had no sense,
I bought a fiddle for eighteen pence,
But the only tune that I could play,
Was ' Over the hills and far away.'

Chorus :
So early in the morning,
So early in the morning,
So early in the morning,
Before the break of day.

When I grew old I thought me wise,
I played my fiddle for the girls and boys,
But the only tune I still could play,
Was ' Over the hills and far away .'

Chorus :

JIGGIDY JIG

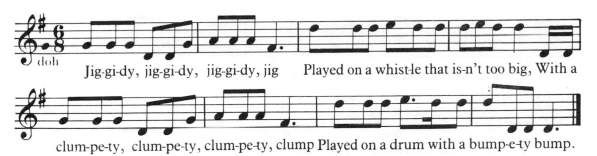

Jig-gi-dy, jig-gi-dy, jig-gi-dy, jig Played on a whist-le that is-n't too big, With a

clum-pe-ty, clum-pe-ty, clum-pe-ty, clump Played on a drum with a bump-e-ty bump.

Jiggidy, jiggidy, jiggidy, jig—
Played on a whistle that isn't too big.
With a clumpety, clumpety, clumpety, clump —
Played on a drum with a bumpety bump.

TUB SCRUB

The old woman must stand
At the tub , tub , tub ,
The dirty clothes
to rub , rub , rub ,
But when they are clean
And fit to be seen,
She'll dress like a lady
And dance on the green.

TERENCE MCDIDDLER

Terence McDiddler
Is a very fine fiddler ,
He'll charm if you please
All the fish from the seas .

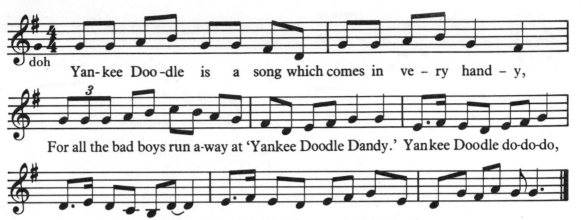

Yan-kee Doo-dle is a song which comes in ve-ry hand-y,

For all the bad boys run a-way at 'Yankee Doodle Dandy.' Yankee Doodle do-do-do,

Yan-kee Doodle Dandy.   All the girls they are so smart and sweet as su-gar can-dy.

Yankee Doodle is a song
Which comes in very handy,
For all the bad boys run away
At ' Yankee Doodle Dandy '.

Yankee Doodle do-do-do-,
Yankee Doodle Dandy ' .
All the girls they are so smart,
And sweet as sugar candy.

GUMMY GOO

Gummy Gummy Goo ,
Half-past-two ,
Shove him in the letter box
And see what'll he do.
I'm telling the nun
You stole a bun,
You put it in your pocket
And you gave me none.

THE LAD

Are you the lad
That hit the lad
The lad around the corner ?
Come here my lad
And tell the lad
That you're the lad
That hit the lad
The lad around the corner .

doh Co-war-dy, co-war-dy, cus – tard, Stick your head in mus – tard.

Cowardy, cowardy, custard,
Stick your head in mustard.

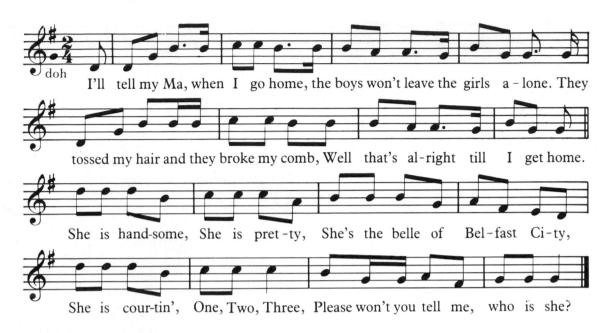

I'll tell my Ma, when I go home, the boys won't leave the girls a-lone. They tossed my hair and they broke my comb, Well that's al-right till I get home. She is hand-some, She is pret-ty, She's the belle of Bel-fast Ci-ty, She is cour-tin', One, Two, Three, Please won't you tell me, who is she?

I'll tell my Ma, when I go home,
The boys won't leave the girls alone,
They tossed my hair and they broke my comb,
Well that's alright till I get home.
She is handsome, she is pretty,
She's the belle of Belfast City,
She is courtin', One, Two, Three,
Please won't you tell me, who is she ?

Albert Mooney says he loves her,
All the boys are fighting for her,
They rap at the door and they ring at the bell,
Saying : ' Oh my true-love, are you well ?'
Out she comes as white as snow,
Rings on her fingers, bells on her toes,
Old Jenny Murphy says she'll die,
If she doesn't get the fellow with the roving eye.

Let the wind and the rain and the hail blow high,
And the snow come shovelling from the sky,
She's as nice as apple pie,
And she'll get her own lad by and by.
When she gets a lad of her own ,
She won't tell her Ma when she gets home.
Let them all come as they will,
But it's Albert Mooney she loves still.

See this finger ?
See this thumb ?
See this fist ?
You'd better run !

ROGUES GO LEOR

From Carrickmacross to Crossmaglen.
There are more rogues than honest men.

DADDY AIKEN

Old Daddy Aiken
Stole a bit of bacon
He put it in his overcoat
For fear it might be taken.

Old Daddy Aiken
Stole another bit of bacon,
He stuffed it up the *chimley*
For fear it might be taken.

THE PIPER'S SON

Tom , Tom , the piper's son,
Stole a pig and away he run.
The pig was ate
And Tom was bate,
And then went roaring down the street.

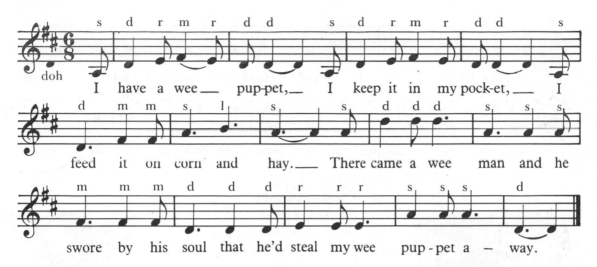

I have a wee — pup-pet, — I keep it in my pock-et, — I feed it on corn and hay. — There came a wee man and he swore by his soul that he'd steal my wee pup-pet a — way.

I have a wee puppet,
I keep it in my pocket,
I feed it on corn and hay.
There came a wee man
And he swore by his soul
That he'd steal my wee puppet away.

John O'Keeffe, he is a thief, He pinched my shoes and la – ces. He took my hat and mit-tens too, And now he's pul – ling fa – ces.

John O'Keeffe
He is a thief,
He pinched my shoes and laces,
He took my hat and mittens too,
And now he's pulling faces.

ROBBERS

See   the rob – bers pas – sing by,   pas – sing by,   pas – sing by, See   the rob-bers pas – sing by,   My   Fair   La – dy.

See the robbers passing by ,
Passing by, passing by,
See the robbers passing by ,
My Fair Lady.

What did the robbers do to you,
Do to you , Do to you ,
What did the robbers do to you,
My Fair Lady .

They stole my watch and stole my chain
Watch and chain, watch and chain,
They stole my watch and stole my chain,
My Fair Lady.

FLYING ELEPHANTS

Can an elephant fly
Way up in the sky ?
No , don't be absurd
That must be a bird ;
Or maybe a bee ,
A fly , or a flea .

doh Too-ral-ly oo-ral-ly oo-ral-ly-ooh, They're looking for monkeys in __ the zoo,

If I had a face like you I'd ap – ply for a si – tu – a – tion.

Toorally oorally oorally ooh,
They're looking for monkeys in the zoo,
If I had a face like you
I'd apply for a situation.

doh

The mon-keys up in the zoo, ___ The mon-keys up in the zoo, ___ Do you

think you could do the things that they do, The mon-keys up in the zoo. ___

The monkeys up in the zoo ,
The monkeys up in the zoo ,
Do you think you could do ,
  The things that they do ,
The monkeys up in the zoo .

MY FRIEND THE KANGAROO

Away up in the zoo
Lives my friend the kangaroo ,
He's very , very small
Though someday I'll find he's tall .
You never hear him grouch
Riding in his mammy's pouch ,
And that's where he's going to stop
Until he learns to hop .

TRUNKS OR TAILS

Elephant, Elephant ,
Clunkety , clunk .
Which is your tail
And which is your trunk ?

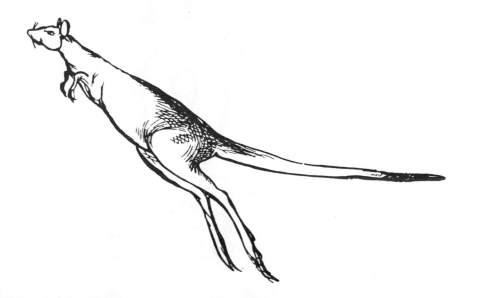

ENVY

Said the monkey to the kangaroo:
' I really wish that I were you -
I'd love to hop and hop and hop
And hop and hop and never stop '.

Said the Kangaroo :
' You wish you were me ?
I'd like to be you
' Way up in a tree '.

THE WISE OLD BIRD

The wise old bird
Sat in the oak,
The more he heard,
The less he spoke,
The less he spoke,
The more he heard,
O wasn't he
The wise old bird.

doh — Lit - tle Ro - bin Red - breast sat up - on a tree,

Up went Pus-sy-cat and down went he. Down came pus-sy and a

way— Ro-bin ran, Says lit - tle Ro-bin Red - breast, 'Catch me if you can.'

Little Robin Redbreast sat upon a tree,
Up went Pussy cat and down went he,
Down came Pussy and away Robin ran,
Says little Robin Redbreast : ' Catch me if you can.'

Little Robin Redbreast jumped upon a wall,
Pussy went after him and nearly took a fall,
Little Robin whistled and what did Pussy say ?
Pussy cat said ' Meow, Meow ', and Robin ran away.

Little Robin Redbreast came to visit me ,
This is what he whistled :
Whistle :
Thank you for my tea !

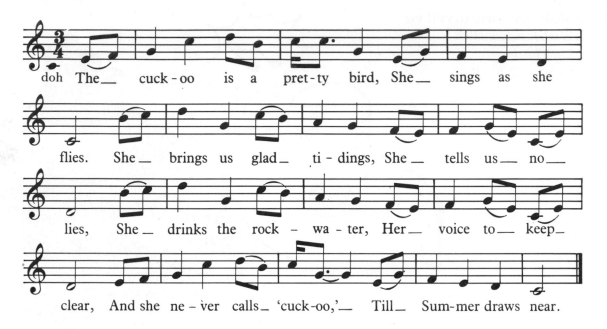

doh The— cuck-oo is a pret-ty bird, She— sings as she
flies. She — brings us glad — ti-dings, She — tells us — no—
lies, She — drinks the rock - wa - ter, Her— voice to — keep—
clear, And she ne – ver calls— 'cuck-oo,'— Till— Sum-mer draws near.

The Cuckoo is a pretty bird ,
She sings as she flies ,
She brings us glad tidings ,
She tell us no lies .
She drinks the rock water ,
Her voice to keep clear ,
And she never calls ' cuck–oo' ,–
Till Summer draws near .

THE OWL

Of all the birds that I did see, The owl is the wi-sest by far to me, For
all day long she sleeps in the tree, And when night comes a-way flies she.

Of all the birds that I did see
The owl is the wisest by far to me.
For all day long she sleeps in the tree,
And when night comes away flies she.

DICKIE BIRDS

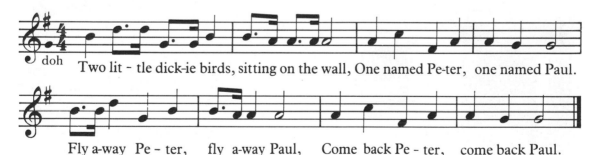

Two lit-tle dick-ie birds, sitting on the wall, One named Pe-ter, one named Paul.
Fly a-way Pe-ter, fly a-way Paul, Come back Pe-ter, come back Paul.

Two little dickie birds, sitting on the wall,
One named Peter, one named Paul.
Fly away Peter, fly away Paul,
Come back Peter, come back Paul.

Mrs Pig a-laying in the mud,
Mrs Pig a-laying in the mud,
Never a worry and never a care,
Mrs Pig she likes it there,
Mrs Pig a-laying in the mud.

FIVE LITTLE PIGS

This little pig has a rub-a-dub,
This little pig has a scrub-a-scrub,
This little piggy ran upstairs,
This little piggy cried out : 'Bears !'
Down came the jar with a mighty slam,
And this little pig ate all the jam.

FOUR LITTLE PIGS

The first little pig broke into the barn,
The second little pig ate all the corn,
The third little pig he hid in the hay,
And the fourth little pig had to pay.

To market to market to buy a fat pig,   Home again, home again, Jig-gi-dy, Jig.   To

mar-ket to mar-ket to   buy a fat hog,   Home again, home again,   Jig-gi-dy Jog.

To market , to market
To buy a fat pig ,
Home again , home again
Jiggidy Jig .
To market to market
To buy a fat hog ,
Home again , home again
Jiggidy Jog .

Whose lit-tle pigs are these? Whose lit-tle pigs are these?— They're

Mickey Mc.Swiggins', They're his little piggins, And I caught them eating my peas.

Whose little pigs are these ?
Whose little pigs are these ?
They're Mickey McSwiggins',
They're his little piggins,
And I caught them eating my peas.

THE OLD PIG

doh I'm an old pig, 'Muc, Muc, Muc', I'm an old pig, 'Muc, Muc, Muc',

Can't sow or dig, 'Muc, Muc, Muc', 'Cos I'm an old pig, 'Muc, Muc, Muc'.

I'm an old pig,
Muc, Muc, Muc.
I'm an old pig,
Muc, Muc, Muc.
Can't sow or dig,
Muc, Muc, Muc.
'Cos I'm an old pig,
Muc, Muc, Muc.

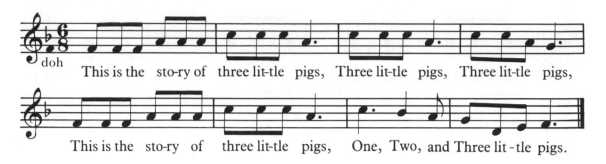

This is the story of three little pigs ,
Three little pigs , three little pigs ,
This is the story of three little pigs -
One , Two , and Three little pigs .

The first little pig made his house out of straw ,
House out of straw , house out of straw ,
The first little pig made his house out of straw .
Straw , straw , his house out of straw .

Big Bad wolf he said : ' Sure I'll blow that house down ,
Blow that house down , blow that house down ',
Big Bad Wolf he said : 'Sure I'll blow that house down ' —
Huff , Puff — And he blew the house down .

The second little pig made his house out of wood ,
House out of wood , house out of wood ,
The second little pig made his house out of wood ,
Wood ,wood , his house out of wood .

Big Bad Wolf he said : ' Sure I'll blow that house down ,
Blow that house down , blow that house down '.
Big Bad Wolf he said : 'Sure I'll blow that house down ' ,
Huff , Puff — And he blew the house down .

The third little pig made his house out of brick ,
House out of brick , house out of brick ,
The third little pig made his house out of brick ,
Brick ,brick , his house out of brick .

Big Bad Wolf he said : ' Sure I'll blow that house down ,
Blow that house down , blow that house down ',
Big Bad Wolf he said : 'Sure I'll blow that house down',
Huff , Puff — He couldn't blow the house down .

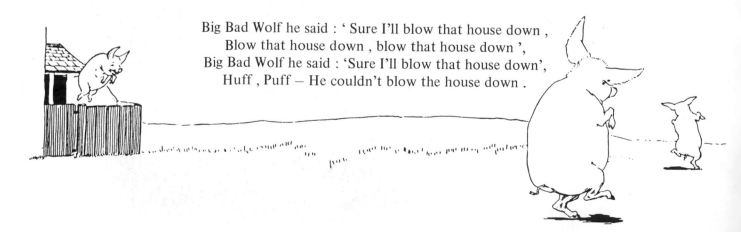

Molly went to Grandpa's farm,
The billy goat chased her round the barn,
Round and round the apple tree,
And this is the song she sang to me :
' I like coffee, I like tea,
  I like you and you like me '.

Chorus :   An Madaírin Rua, Rua, Rua, Rua, Rua,
           An Madaírin Rua tá granna,
           An Madaírin Rua 'Na lui'sa luachair
           'S barr a dha chluis in áirde.

           The little red fox is a raider sly,
           In the misty morning creeping,
           With a morsel to his taste, he hurries off in haste,
           While the farmyard's soundly sleeping.

Chorus

A duck, says he, has charms for me,
Likewise a good cock crowing,
But a fine fat goose is most of use,
To a family young and growing.

Chorus

MITTY MATTY

Mit-ty Mat-ty had a hen, She lays eggs for gent-le-men,
Some-times nine and some-times ten, Mit-ty Mat-ty had a hen.

Mitty Matty had a hen,
She lays eggs for gentlemen,
Sometimes nine and sometimes ten,
Mitty Matty had a hen.

TEDDY BEAR

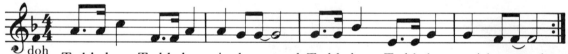

Teddy bear, Teddy bear, tip the ground, Teddy bear, Teddy bear, twirl a-round.

Teddy Bear, Teddy Bear, tip the ground,
Teddy Bear, Teddy Bear, twirl around,
Teddy Bear, Teddy Bear, show your shoe,
Teddy Bear, Teddy Bear, that will do.
Teddy Bear, Teddy Bear, climb the stairs,
Teddy Bear, Teddy Bear, say your prayers.
Teddy Bear, Teddy Bear, turn off the light,
Teddy Bear, Teddy Bear, say 'Goodnight'

. . . . .Goodnight.

One day of late I had the luck, To meet up with my friend the duck, She swims the sea, she flies the air, She wad-dles here and wad-dles there. Said I 'My friend, you're real-ly free, You fly the air__ and swim the sea, And to walk on land you have the knack,' The duck she smiled and she said 'QUACK, QUACK.'

One day of late I had the luck
To meet up with my friend the duck,
She swims the sea, she flies the air,
She waddles here and waddles there.

Said I ' My friend you're really free,
You fly the air and swim the sea,
And to walk on land you have the knack,'
The duck she smiled and said ' QUACK QUACK.'

ROUND AND ROUND THE GARDEN

Round and round the garden
Like a Teddy Bear ,
One step ,
Two steps ,
And tickley under there .

THE FLY CATCHER

Ask no questions ,
Tell no lies ,
If you open your mouth
DON'T swallow the flies !

THE ANIMAL CHORUS

Bow-wow, said the dog,
And meow, said the cat.
Grunt, grunt, said the pig,
And squeek, went the rat.
Caw-caw, said the crow,
Quack, quack, said the duck,
And the cuckoo, you know . . . . .
COOOOO – KOOOOO.

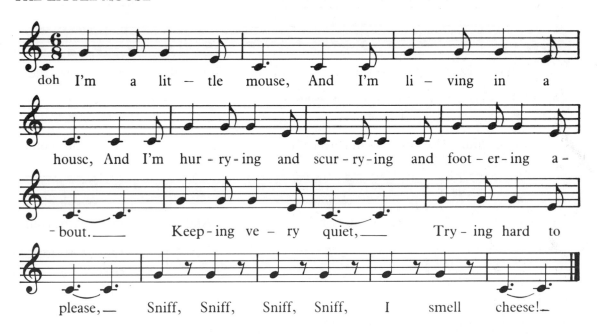

doh I'm a lit—tle mouse, And I'm li—ving in a house, And I'm hur—ry—ing and scur—ry—ing and foot—er—ing a—bout.___ Keep—ing ve—ry quiet,___ Try—ing hard to please,— Sniff, Sniff, Sniff, Sniff, I smell cheese!—

I'm a little mouse
And I'm living in a house,
And I'm hurrying and scurrying
And footering about.
Keeping very quiet,
Trying hard to please,
Sniff, Sniff, Sniff, Sniff,
I smell cheese !

THE BEAR WENT OVER THE MOUNTAIN

doh | The Bear went o-ver the moun-tain, The Bear went o-ver the moun-tain, The Bear went o-ver the moun-tain, To see what he could see. —— And what do you think he could see? —— And what do you think he could see?—— The o-ther side of the moun-tain, The o-ther side of the moun-tain, The o-ther side of the moun-tain, O that's what he could see. —

The Bear went over the mountain,
The Bear went over the mountain,
The Bear went over the mountain,
To see what he could see.

And what do you think he could see ?
And what do you think he could see ?

The other side of the mountain,
The other side of the mountain,
The other side of the mountain,
O that's what he could see.

doh

Pus – sy got the meas – les on the first day of

Spring, __ The first day of Spring, __ The first day of

Spring. __ Pus – sy got the meas – les on the first day of

Spring, __ The poor, __ The poor, __ The poor wee thing. __

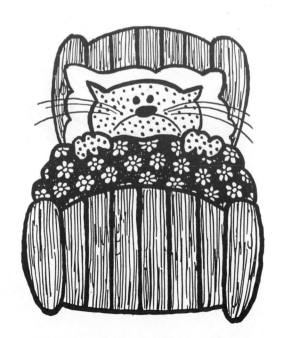

Pussy got the measles
on the first day of Spring ,
The first day of Spring ,
The first day of Spring .
Pussy got the measles
on the first day of Spring ,
The poor ,
The poor ,
The poor wee thing .

doh

It – sy Bit – sy spi – der, climb-ing up the spout, ___

Down came the rain, ___ And washed the spi – der out. ___

Out came the sun - shine, And dried up all the rain. ___

It – sy bit – sy spi – der, Climb-ing up a – gain. ___

Itsy Bitsy spider ,
Climbing up the spout ,
Down came the rain
And washed the spider out .
Out came the sunshine
And dried up all the rain .
Itsy Bitsy spider
Climbing up again .

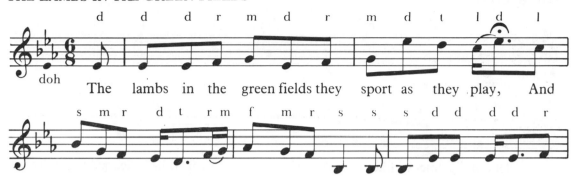

The lambs in the green fields they sport as they play, And

lots of straw-ber-ries grow round the salt sea, And lots of straw-ber-ries grow

round the salt sea, And ma-ny's the ship sails the o-cean.

The lambs in the green fields they sport as they play ,
And lots of strawberries grow round the salt sea ,
And lots of strawberries grow round the salt sea .
And many's the ship sails the ocean .

s d m s m f r m s
doh
The cat went wild and jumped a – bout, She

d d m s d r r m r r s d m s m
let out a 'meow' like a ter – ri –ble shout, Leaped here, leaped there, leaped

f r m s d d m s d d d r d d
all a – round, She pranced in the air and she rolled on the ground.

The cat went wild and jumped about,
She let out a 'meow' like a terrible shout,
Leaped here, leaped there, leaped all around,
She pranced in the air and she rolled on the ground.

KILKENNY CATS

There were two cats of Kilkenny ,
Each thought there was one cat too many ,
So they fought and they fit ,
And they scratched and they bit ,
Till , excepting their nails
And the tips of their tails ,
Instead of two cats , there weren't any .

I wish I had the shep-herd's lamb, I wish I had the shepherd's lamb, I wish I had the shepherd's lamb, And Kitty coming af-ter, Is Ó goirim goirim thú, Is grá mo chroí gan cheilig thu, Is Ó goir-im goir-im thú, 'S peat-a beag do mhat-har.

I wish I had the shepherd's lamb ,
I wish I had the shepherd's lamb ,
I wish I had the shepherd's lamb ,
And Kitty coming after .

Chorus :

Is Ó goirim goirim thú ,
Is grá mo chroí gan cheilig thú ,
Is Ó goirim goirim thú ,
' S tú peata beag do mháthar .

I wish I had a yellow cow ,
I wish I had a yellow cow ,
I wish I had a yellow cow ,
And welcome from my darling .

Chorus :

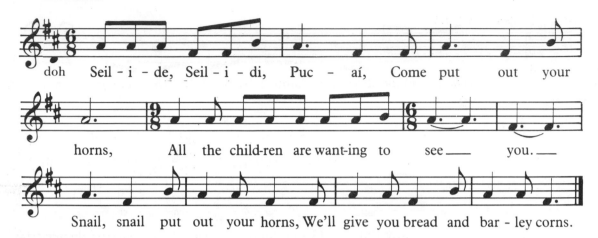

doh Seil - i - de, Seil - i - di, Puc - aí, Come put out your

horns, All the child-ren are want-ing to see ___ you. ___

Snail, snail put out your horns, We'll give you bread and bar - ley corns.

Seilide Seilide pucaí
Come put out your horns ,
All the children are
wanting to see you.

Snail , snail ,
put out your horns ,
We'll give you bread
and barley corns .

BINN BEAGLES

Upper Binn beagles,
Lower Binn brocks,
Killycor capons,
and Claudy game cocks.

DOWN ON THE CARPET

Down on the carpet you shall kneel ,
While the green grass grows at your feet ,
Stand up straight upon you feet ,
And choose the one you love so sweet .

Now you are married , life enjoy —
First a girl and then a boy ;
Seven years after , seven years to come ,
Fire on the mountains , run boys run .

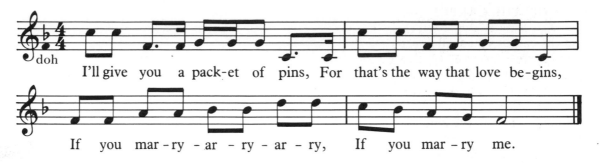

I'll give you a pack-et of pins, For that's the way that love be-gins,

If you mar-ry – ar – ry – ar – ry, If you mar-ry me.

I'll give you a packet of pins ,
For that's the way that love begins ,
If you marry-arry-arry ,
If you marry me .

I don't want you packet of pins ,
If that's the way that love begins ,
I won't marry-arry-arry ,
I won't marry you .

I'll give you a dress of red ,
All stitched round with a silver thread ,
If you marry-arry-arry ,
If you marry me .

I don't want your dress of red ,
All stitched round with a silver thread ,
I won't marry-arrry-arrry ,
I won't marry you .

I'll give you a wooden spoon ,
To feed the baby in the afternoon .
If you marry-arry-arry ,
If you marry me .

I don't want your wooden spoon ,
To feed the baby in the afternoon ,
I won't marry-arry-arry ,
I won't marry you .

I'll give you the keys to my chest ,
And all the money that I possess ,
If you marry-arry-arry ,
If you marrry me .

Yes I'll take the keys of your chest ,
And all the money that you possess ,
Yes I'll marry-arry-arry ,
Yes I'll marry you.

O dear me , you're very funny ,
You don't love me, you love my money ,
But I'll not marry-arry-arry ,
I'll not marry you .

THE LONGLEGGEDS

Did you ever ever ever
In your long legged life
Meet a long legged man
And his long legged wife ?
No, I never never never
In my long legged life
Met a long legged man
With his long legged wife.

doh

In and out the win-dows, In and out the win-dows,

In and out the win-dows, As you have done be – fore.

In and out the windows,
In and out the windows,
In and out the windows,
As you have done before.

Kneel before your lover,
Kneel before your lover,
Kneel before your lover,
As you have done before.

APPLES AND PEARS

doh

I love an ap-ple and I love a pear, I love the lass with the long yellow hair.

Still I love her, I'll for-give her, I'll go with her, Wher-ev-er she goes.

I love an apple ,
And I love a pear ,
I love the lass
With the long yellow hair .

Chorus :

Still I love her ,
I'll forgive her ,
I'll go with her
Wherever she goes .

She gave me a hankie ,
Its colour was blue .
Before I could use it
She tore it in two .

Chorus :

There's tea in the tea pot
And bread on the shelf ,
If you want anymore
You can sing it yourself .

Chorus :

COURTING IN THE KITCHEN

doh Come sin-gle beau and belle, And give me your at-ten-tion. Don't

e-ver fall in love, 'Tis the di-vil's own in-ven-tion. For

once in love I fell, With a maid-en's smile be-witch-ing, Miss

Hen-ri-et-ta Bell, Down in Cap-tain Kel-ly's kit-chen. Ri-

-toor-al-oor-aye-a, Ri-toor-al-oor-aye-ad-dy, Ri-

-toor-al-oor-aye-a, With me fad-dle-o-me-dad-dy.

Come single beau and belle ,
And give me your attention .
Don't ever fall in love ,
Tis the divil's own invention .
For once in love I fell
With a maiden's smile bewitching ,
Miss Henrietta Bell
Down in Captain Kelly's kitchen .
Ri—toor—al—oor—aye—a ,
Ri—toor—al—oor—aye—addy ,
Ri—toor—al—oor—aye—a ,
With me faddle—o—me—daddy .

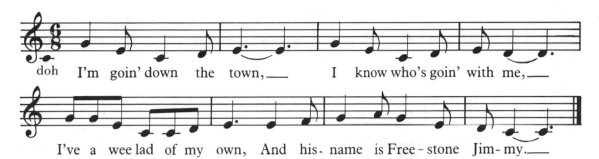

doh I'm goin' down the town, __ I know who's goin' with me, __

I've a wee lad of my own, And his name is Free-stone Jim-my. __

I'm goin' down the town,
I know who's goin' with me,
I've a wee lad of my own
And his name is Freestone Jimmy.
He wears a big top hat,
And his waistcoat's in the fashion,
But he has to stay in bed
'Cos his Sunday shirt is washin',
Some do say he's bold,
But others say he's bonny,
And he's the lad for me,
And his name is Freestone Jimmy.

THE FARMER WANTS A WIFE

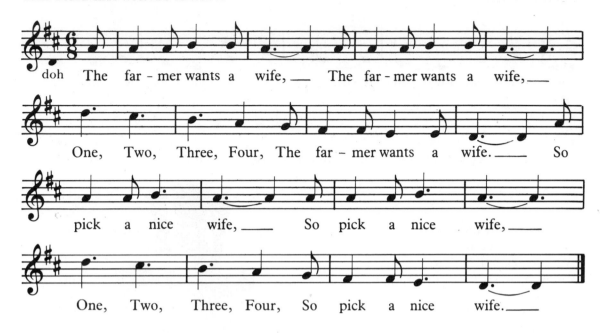

doh | The far-mer wants a wife, — The far-mer wants a wife, —

One, Two, Three, Four, The far-mer wants a wife. — So

pick a nice wife, — So pick a nice wife, —

One, Two, Three, Four, So pick a nice wife. —

The farmer wants a wife, the farmer wants a wife,
1, 2, 3, 4, the farmer wants a wife.

So pick a nice wife, so pick a nice wife,
1, 2, 3, 4, so pick a nice wife.

The wife wants a child, the wife wants a child,
1, 2, 3, 4, the wife wants a child.

The child wants a nurse, the child wants a nurse,
1, 2, 3, 4, the child wants a nurse.

So pick a nice nurse, so pick a nice nurse,
1, 2, 3, 4, so pick a nice nurse.

The nurse wants a dog, the nurse wants a dog,
1, 2, 3, 4, the nurse wants a dog.

So pick a nice dog, so pick a nice dog,
1, 2, 3, 4, so pick a nice dog.

The dog wants a bone, the dog wants a bone,
1, 2, 3, 4, the dog wants a bone.

So pick a nice bone, so pick a nice bone,
1, 2, 3, 4, so pick a nice bone.

The bone's left alone, the bone's left alone,
1, 2, 3, 4, the bone's left alone.

doh | John-ny, love-ly John-ny, Do— you mind the day? You—
came to my win-dow to— lead— me a — way. You—
said you would mar-ry me, A-bove all— fe — male— kind,
John-ny, love-ly John-ny, What has al-tered your mind?

Johnny, lovely Johnny ,
Do you mind the day ?
You came to my window
To lead me away .
You said you would marry me
Above all female kind ,
Johnny ,lovely Johnny ,
What has altered your mind ?

doh On the banks of the Ro – ses, My love and I sat down, And

I took out my vi - o-lin, To play my love a tune. In the mid-dle of the tune, She

turned and she said: 'Ar-rah, John-ny, Love-ly John-ny, Would you leave me'.

On the banks of the Roses
My love and I sat down ,
And I took out my violin
To play my love a tune .
In the middle of the tune
She turned and she said :
' Arrah Johnny , Lovely Johnny ,
Would you leave me ? '

And if ever I get married
' Twill be in the month of May ,
When the leaves they are green
And the meadows they are gay .
And I and my true love
Will laugh and sport and play
On the bonny , bonny , banks
of the Roses .

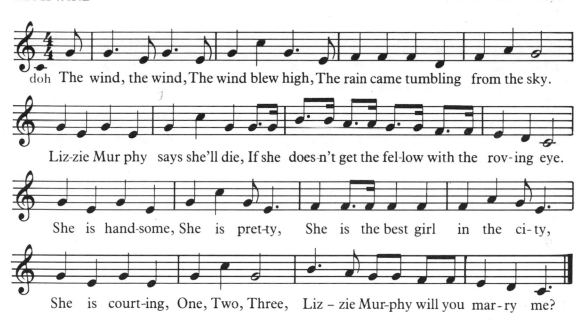

doh The wind, the wind, The wind blew high, The rain came tumbling from the sky.

Liz-zie Mur-phy says she'll die, If she does-n't get the fel-low with the rov-ing eye.

She is hand-some, She is pret-ty, She is the best girl in the ci-ty,

She is court-ing, One, Two, Three, Liz – zie Mur-phy will you mar-ry me?

The wind , the wind ,
The wind blew high ,
The rain came tumbling from the sky .
Lizzie Murphy says she'll die
If she doesn't get the fellow with the roving eye .

She is handsome , she is pretty ,
She's the best girl in the city ,
She is courting , One , Two , Three ,
Lizzie Murphy will you marry me ?

I MARRIED A WIFE

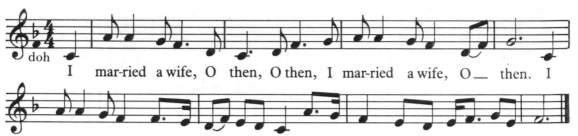

married a wife, She's the bane of my life Sure the world must be coming to an end.

I married a wife,
O then, O then,
I married a wife,
O then,
I married a wife,
She's the bane of my life —
Sure the world must be coming to an end.

I sent her down for cheese,
O then, O then,
I sent her down for cheese,
O then,
I sent her down for cheese,
And she fell and skinned her knees —
Sure the world must be coming to an end.

I sent her down for cabbage,
O then, O then,
I sent her down for cabbage,
O then,
I sent her down for cabbage
And she ate it like a savage —
Sure the world must be coming to an end.

I sent her down for bread,
O then, O then,
I sent her down for bread,
O then,
I sent her down for bread
And she fell down dead —
Sure the world must be coming to an end.

I married another,
O then, O then,
I married another,
O then,
I married another,
She was worse than the other —
Sure the world must be coming to an end.

MY DAD

My Dad he has a hairy chest,
My Dad he wears a woollen vest,
He always smokes his dirty pipe,
In the morning, evening and the night.
He went up North the other day,
And brought me home a Milky Way,
But when he goes I'm always sad,
Because he is the greatest Dad.

Sez— my ould one to   your ould one: 'Will you   come to the Wax-ies'
Dar-gle', Sez— your ould one to   my ould one; 'I   have-n't got a   far-del.

Sez my ould one to your ould one :
' Will you come to the Waxies' Dargle ? '
Says your ould one to my ould one :
' I haven't got a fardel'.

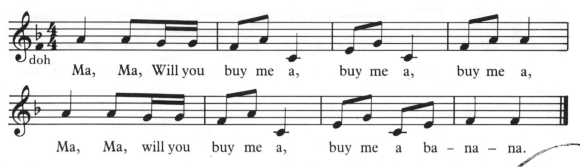

Ma, Ma, Will you buy me a, buy me a, buy me a,

Ma, Ma, will you buy me a, buy me a ba – na – na.

Ma , Ma , will you buy me a ,
　Buy me a , buy me a ,
Ma , Ma , will you buy me a ,
　Buy me a banana .

Yes my child I'll buy you a ,
　Buy you a , buy you a ,
Yes my child I'll buy you a ,
　Buy you a banana .

Ma , Ma , will you peel the skin ,
　Peel the skin , peel the skin ,
Ma , Ma ,will you peel the skin ,
　The skin of my banana .

Yes my child I'll peel the skin ,
　Peel the skin , peel the skin ,
Yes my child I'll peel the skin ,
　The skin of your banana .

Ma , Ma , do you want a bite ,
　Want a bite , want a bite ,
Ma ,Ma , do you want a bite ,
　A bite of my banana .

Yes my child I want a bite ,
　Want a bite , want a bite ,
Yes my child I want a bite ,
　A bite of your banana .

Ma , Ma , you're a greedy thing ,
A greedy thing , a greedy thing ,
Ma , Ma , you're a greedy thing ,
　You ate all my banana .

doh

Oh, our wee school is a nice wee school, It's made of bricks and

plas - ter, And all that's wrong with our wee school is the bald - y head-ed

mas - ter. He goes to the pub on a Sat-ur-day night, He goes to church on

Sun-day. He prays to God to give him might, To bat -ter us on Mon-day.

Oh our wee school is a nice wee school ,
It's made of bricks and plaster ,
And all that's wrong with our wee school
Is the baldy headed master .

He goes to the pub on a Saturday night ,
He goes to church on Sunday ,
He prays to God to give him might
To batter us on Monday .

doh Gran-ny, Gran-ny, Grey,___ Can we go out to play?___ We

won't go near the wa – ter, Or chase the ducks a – way.

Granny, Granny, Grey,
Can we go out to play ?
We won't go near the water,
Or chase the ducks away.

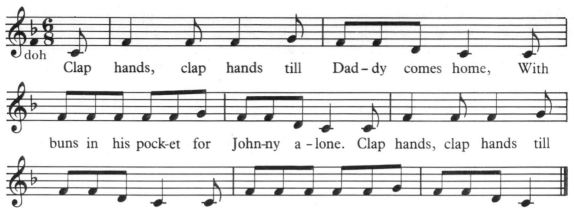

doh

Clap hands, clap hands till Dad-dy comes home, With

buns in his pock-et for John-ny a-lone. Clap hands, clap hands till

Dad-dy comes home, For Dad-dy has mo-ney and Mam-my has none.

Clap hands, clap hands,
Till Daddy comes home,
With buns in his pocket
For Johnny alone.

Clap hands, clap hands,
Till Daddy comes home,
For Daddy has money
And Mammy has none.

DESPERATE DAN

doh Dan, Dan, the sil-ly old man, Washed his face in a fry-ing pan,

Brushed his hair with the gar-den rake, And combed his beard with a bo-ney old hake.

Dan, Dan, the silly old man
Washed his face in a frying pan,
Brushed his hair with the garden rake
And combed his beard with a boney old hake.

Oh, you can-ny shove your gran-ny off a bus, Oh, you canny shove your gran-ny off a bus, Oh, you can-ny shove your granny, 'Cos she's your mammy's mammy, Oh, you can-ny shove your gran-ny off a bus.

Oh you canny shove your granny off a bus ,
Oh you canny shove your granny off a bus ,
Oh you canny shove your granny
'Cos she's you mammy's mammy ,
Oh you canny shove your granny off a bus .

You can shove your other granny off a bus ,
You can shove your other granny off a bus ,
You can shove your other granny
' Cos she's you daddy's Mammy ,
You can shove your other granny off a bus .

doh Fish fid-dle-dee – dee, My Aunt – ie caught a flea, She roast – ed it, and toast – ed it, And ate it for her tea.

Fish fiddle dee dee ,
My Auntie caught a flea ,
She roasted it
And toasted it
And ate it for her tea .

MOTHERS

When my mother and your mother
Were hanging out the clothes ,
My mother gave you mother
A punch on the nose .

MAMMY, DADDY, UNCLE DICK

Mammy , Daddy , Uncle Dick ,
Went to Dublin on a stick ,
The stick broke ,
What a joke ,
Mammy , Daddy ,Uncle Dick .

APRIL FOOL

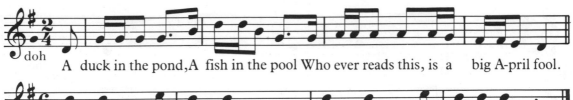

A duck in the pond, A fish in the pool Who ever reads this, is a big A-pril fool.

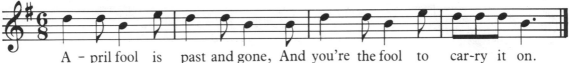

A - pril fool is past and gone, And you're the fool to car-ry it on.

A duck in the pond,
A fish in the pool —
Whoever reads this
Is a big April fool.

But April Fool is past and gone,
And you're the fool to carry it on.

HOT CROSS BUNS (Good Friday)

Hot Cross Buns, Hot Cross Buns, One a pen-ny, Two a penny, Hot Cross Buns.

Hot Cross Buns,
Hot Cross Buns,
One a penny,
Two a penny,
Hot Cross Buns.

Hot Cross Buns,
Hot Cross Buns,
If your daughters
Do not like them,
Give them to your sons.

Daf - fo - dil - lies yel - low, ___ Daf - fo - dil - lies gay,

Put them on the ta - ble on East - er ___ day.

Daffodillies yellow,
Daffodillies gay,
Put them on the table
On Easter Day.

doh Hal – low – een is come, And the geese are get – ting fat,

Please put a pen – ny in the old man's hat. If you

have-n't got a pen-ny, ___ A ha'-pen-ny will do. If you

have-n't got a ha' – pen – ny God bless you!

Hallowe'en is come
And the geese are getting fat,
Please put a penny
In the blind man's hat.
If you haven't got a penny,
A ha'penny will do,
If you haven't got a ha'penny,
God bless you !

Hallowe'en is past
And the geese are getting thin,
Please put a penny
In the old man's tin.
If you haven't got a penny,
A ha'penny will do,
If you haven't got a ha'penny,
God bless you !

PLAY PINS (Christmas Game)

Pippity poppety play me a pin ,
Open the door to let me in .
Let me lose or let me win ,
This is the hand the pin lies in .

THE WREN BOYS' SONG (St Stephen's Day)

doh

The wren, the wren, The King of all birds, On

Ste – phen's Day was caught in the furze, Though he was lit-tle, His

ho-nour was great, So give us a pen-ny to give us a treat. *(trate)*

The wren , the wren , the king of all birds
On Stephen's Day was caught in the furze ,
Though he was little his honour was great ,
So give us a penny to give us a treat .

My box would speak if it had a tongue ,
And two or three coppers can do it no wrong ,
Sing holly , sing ivy , sing ivy , sing holly ,
A drop just to drink it would drown melancholy .

And if you draw it of the best
I hope in heaven your soul may rest ,
But if you draw it of the small ,
It won't agree with the Wrenboys at all .

Missus you're a very fine woman ,
A very fine woman , a very fine woman ,
Missus you're a very fine woman ,
You gave us a penny to bury the wren .

THE BELFAST BOY

There's a boy in the town of Belfast
Whose trousers are always half-mast,
If he stretched them a foot,
They'd reach down to his boot,
And he'd cover his ankles at last.

THE FELLOW FROM DONEGAL

A fellow from Donegal
Once went to a fancy-dress ball.
He appeared as a bun
And he thought it great fun,
Till a dog ate him up in the hall.

THE RATHCOOLE LAD

There was a young lad from Rathcoole,
Who decided he'd not go to school,
When his teacher was told,
She said he was bold,
For what she called playing the fool.

THE YOUNG GIRL FROM TRALEE

There was a young girl from Tralee,
Who ate an old boot for her tea,
At once she got sick
So the doctor came quick,
But the laces were all he could see.

THE YOUNG FELLOW FROM GLIN

There was a young fellow from Glin,
Who was most remarkably thin,
You would hear his da roar :
'Could you eat a bit more ?
Before you fall out of your skin ! '

RIDDLE ME THIS

Riddle me this
And riddle me that —
It's over you head
And under your hat . . . . . .

your hair .

PUNCH AND JUDY

Punch and Judy ran a race
Round and round the fireplace ,
Judy stopped to tie her lace ,
Who won ?
PUNCH . . . . Ouch !

HOPPER

I hop on the ground ,
But I'm not easily found ,
My colour is green ,
In the water I'm seen .
What am I ? . . . .

BETTY BOTTER

Betty Botter bought some butter,
'But' she said, ' The butter's bitter,
If I put it in my batter
It will make my batter bitter.
But a bit of better butter
That will make my batter better'.
So she bought a bit of butter
Better than her bitter butter,
And she put it in her batter
And the batter was not bitter.
So 'twas better Betty Botter
Bought a bit of better butter.

WEE WIGGIE

Wee Wiggie
Poke Piggie
Tom Whistle
John Gristle
And old grey
GOBBLE GOBBLE GOBBLE

SEA SHELLS

She sells sea shells on the sea shore ,
The shells that she sells are sea shells I'm sure ,
So if she sells sea shells on the sea shore ,
I'm sure that the shells are sea shore shells .

SHE SHELLS SEASELLS BY THE SHESHORE
SEASORE SHOSH....BEACH !!

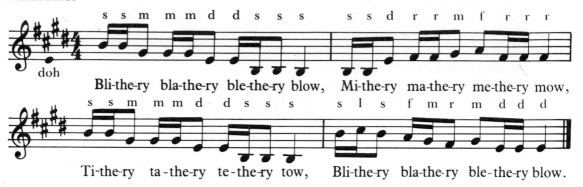

ssmmmddsss   ssdrrmfrrr

doh

Bli-the-ry bla-the-ry ble-the-ry blow, Mi-the-ry ma-the-ry me-the-ry mow,

ssmmmddsss   slsfmrmddd

Ti-the-ry ta-the-ry te-the-ry tow, Bli-the-ry bla-the-ry ble-the-ry blow.

Blithery blathery blethery blow,
Mithery mathery methery mow,
Tithery tathery tethery tow,
Blithery blathery blethery blow.

HOW MUCH WOOD ?

How much wood
Would a woodpecker peck
If a woodpecker could peck wood ?
A woodpecker would peck
As much wood as a woodpecker could,
If a woodpecker could peck wood.

How much oil
Would a gumboil boil
If a gumboil could boil oil ?
A gumboil would boil
As much oil as a gumboil could boil,
If a gumboil could boil oil .

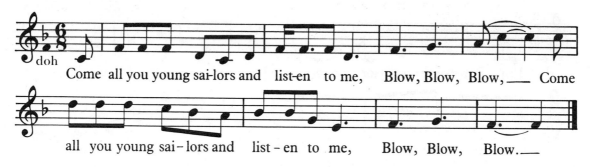

Come all you young sai-lors and list-en to me, Blow, Blow, Blow, ___ Come all you young sai-lors and list-en to me, Blow, Blow, Blow. ___

Come all you young sailors and listen to me ,
Blow , blow , blow ,
Come all you young sailors and listen to me ,
Blow , blow , blow .

This is the song we sing on the sea ,
Blow , blow , blow ,
This is the song we sing on the sea ,
Blow , blow , blow .

Our good ship is sailing from old Dublin town ,
Blow , blow , blow .
Our good ship is sailing from old Dublin town ,
Blow , blow , blow .

We're off and away for the sweet Cobh of Cork ,
Blow , blow , blow,
If we turn the wrong way we'll end up in New York ,
Blow , blow , blow .

POPEYE THE SAILORMAN

doh I'm Pop-eye the sai - lor man, — I live in a car - a - van, — I

o -pened the door, And I fell on the floor, I'm Pop-eye the sai - lor - man. —

I'm Popeye the sailor man ,
I live in a caravan ,
I opened the door
And I fell on the floor ,
I'm Popeye the sailor man .

I'm Popeye the sailor man ,
Way off in the sea of Japan ,
I sat in a boat
But the Yoke wouldn't float ,
I'm Popeye the sailor man .

LITTLE TEE—WEE

Little Tee-Wee
Went to sea ,
All in a pea-green boat .
The boat bended -
My story's ended .

A BIG SHIP SAILING

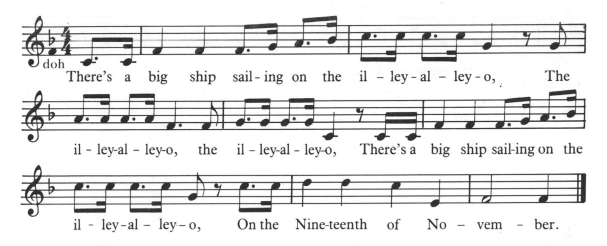

There's a big ship sail-ing on the il – ley-al – ley-o, The il – ley-al – ley-o, the il – ley-al-ley-o, There's a big ship sail-ing on the il – ley-al – ley-o, On the Nine-teenth of No – vem – ber.

There's a big ship sailing on the illey-alley-o,
The illey-alley-o, the illey-alley-o,
There's a big ship sailing on the illey-alley-o,
On the Nineteenth of November.

There's a big ship sailing rocking on the sea,
Rocking on the sea, rocking on the sea,
There's a big ship sailing rocking on the sea,
On the Nineteenth of November.

There's a big ship sailing back again,
Back again, back again,
There's a big ship sailing back again,
On the Nineteenth of November.

THE BANGOR BOAT

The Ban-gor boat's a - way, ___ I can no long-er stay, ___

SPOKEN

One o'clock, Two o'clock, Three o'clock and a - way.

The Bangor boat's away,
I can no longer stay,
One o'clock, two o'clock,
Three o'clock and away.

SALT SEA SAILOR

A sai-lor went to sea, sea, sea, To see what he could see, see, see, But

all that he could see, see, see, Was the bot-tom of the deep blue sea, sea, sea.

A sailor went to sea, sea, sea,
To see what he could see, see, see,
But all that he could see, see, see,
Was the bottom of the deep blue sea, sea, sea.

BOBBY SHAFTO

Bobby Shafto's gone to sea, —
Silver buckles on his knee, —
He'll come back and marry me, —
Bonny Bobby Shafto.

Bobby Shafto's fat and fair,
Combing down his yellow hair,
He's my lad for evermore,
Bonny Bobby Shafto.

Bobby Shafto walking out,
all his ribbons fly about,
All the lassies give a shout,
Bonny Bobby Shafto.

Bobby Shafto's gone to sea,
Silver buckles on his knee,
He'll come back and marry me,
Bonny Bobby Shafto .

Bobby Shafto's fat and fair,
Combing down his yellow hair,
He's my lad for evermore,
Bonny Bobby Shafto.

Bobby Shafto walking out,
All his ribbons fly about,
All the lassies give a shout,
Bonny Bobby Shafto.

THE COBBLER

Is Johnny in ?
Yes he is !
Can he mend a shoe ?
Yes , one or two .
Here's a nail ,
There's a nail ,
Tick Tack Too .

JOHNSTON, MOONEY AND O' BRIEN

Johnston , Mooney , and O'Brien
Bought a horse for one-and nine ,
When the horse began to kick
Johnston Mooney bought a stick .
When the stick began to break ,
Johnston Mooney bought a rake .
When the rake began to smart
Johnston Mooney bought a cart .

FRESH HERRINGS

Be not sparing ,
Leave off swearing ,
Buy my herring
Fresh from Malahide ,
Better never was tried ,
Come and eat them with fresh butter and mustard ,
Their bellies are soft and as white as custard .
Come , sixpence a dozen , to get me some bread ,
Or , like my own herrings , I soon shall be dead .

Dean Swift

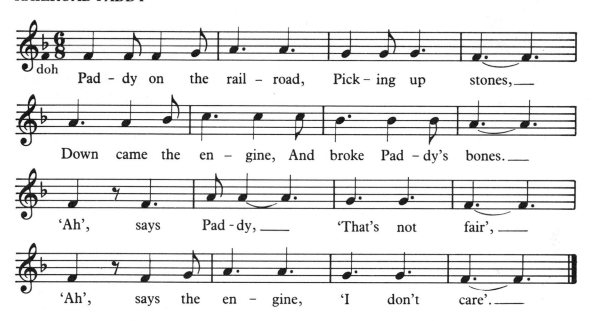

Paddy on the railroad, Picking up stones, __ Down came the en-gine, And broke Pad-dy's bones. __ 'Ah', says Pad-dy, __ 'That's not fair', __ 'Ah', says the en-gine, 'I don't care'. __

Paddy on the railroad
Picking up stones
Down came the engine
And broke Paddy's bones .
Ah , says Paddy ,
That's not fair ,
Ah ,says the engine ,
I don't care .

doh
I'm a ro-ving Jack, a ram-bling Jack, A rov-ing Jack of all _ trades, And if you want to know my name, They call me Jack of all trades.

I'm a roving Jack, a rambling Jack,
A roving Jack of all trades,
And if you want to know my name,
They call me Jack of all trades.

THE SHOEMAKER

I'm a shoemaker to trade,
I'll work in rainy weather,
Oh I have made two pair today,
From a side and a half of leather.

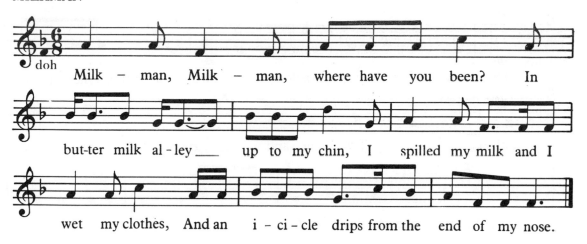

Milkman, milkman, where have you been ?
In buttermilk alley up to my chin,
I spilled my milk and I wet my clothes,
And an icicle drips from the end of my nose.

doh One man shall mow my mea-dow, ____ Two men shall ga-ther it to-geth-er, ____ Two men and one more, Shall shear my ewes and rams and lambs, ___ And gath-er my fold to - geth-er. ____

One man shall mow my meadow ,
Two men shall gather it together ,
Two men and one more
Shall shear my ewes and rams and lambs ,
And gather my fold together .

SMITH THE FARRIER

Jack Smith of Munterlony ,
Tell me , can you shoe this pony ?
Yes indeed for that I can ,
As well as any other man :
Here's a nail , and there's a prod ,
Now your pony is well shod .

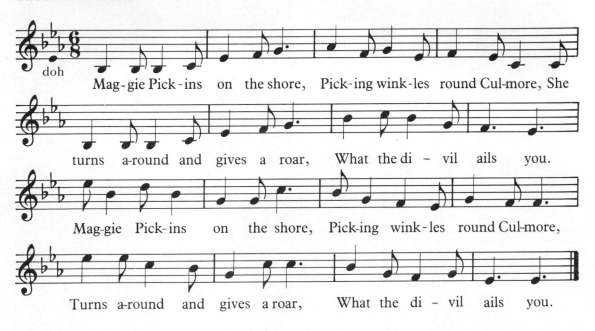

doh

Mag-gie Pick-ins on the shore, Pick-ing wink-les round Cul-more, She
turns a-round and gives a roar, What the di – vil ails you.
Mag-gie Pick-ins on the shore, Pick-ing wink-les round Cul-more,
Turns a-round and gives a roar, What the di – vil ails you.

Maggie Pickins on the shore ,
Picking winkles round Culmore ,
She turns around and gives a roar ,
What the divil ails you .
(repeat).

Rub-a-dub-dub ,
Three men in a tub ,
The butcher , the baker , the candlestick maker ,
They all jumped out of a rotten potato .

You're in the ar-my now, ___ And not be-hind the plough. ___ You'll

ne-ver get rich,   Dig-ging a ditch You're in   the ar-my now. ___

You're in the army now
And not behind the plough .
You'll never get rich
Digging a ditch —
You're in the army now .

SALLY WALKER

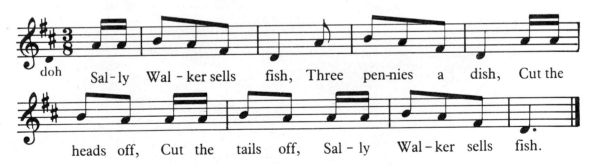

Sal-ly Wal-ker sells   fish, Three pen-nies   a   dish,   Cut the

heads off,   Cut the   tails off,   Sal-ly   Wal-ker sells   fish.

Sally Walker sell fish ,
Three pennies a dish ,
Cut the heads off ,
Cut the tails off ,
Sally Walker sells fish .

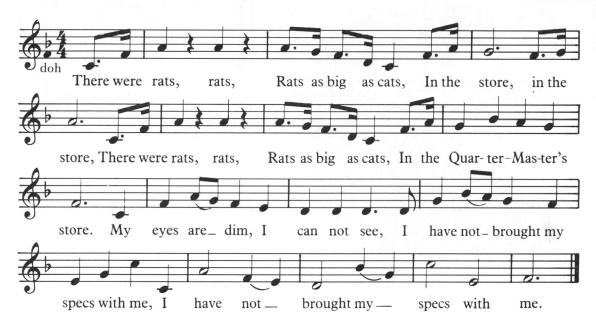

There were rats, rats, Rats as big as cats, In the store, in the store, There were rats, rats, Rats as big as cats, In the Quar-ter-Mas-ter's store. My eyes are— dim, I can not see, I have not— brought my specs with me, I have not — brought my — specs with me.

There were rats, rats,
Rats as big as cats
In the store, in the store,
There were rats, rats,
Rats as big as cats
In the Quartermaster's store.

My eyes are dim, I cannot see,
I have not brought my specs with me,
I have not brought my specs with me.

THE SPANISH KNIGHT

Here is one knight has come from Spain ,
A-courting of your daughter Jane ,
My daughter Jane is far too young ,
She can't abide you flattering tongue :
Go home go home your flattering tongue :
And scour your spurs till they grow bright .
My spurs , my spurs , they owe you nought ,
For in your land they were not bought ;
Then fare you well my lady gay ,
I'll go and court some other way .
Come back , cone back , you Spanish Knight
And choose the one you love so bright .

FAIR ROSA

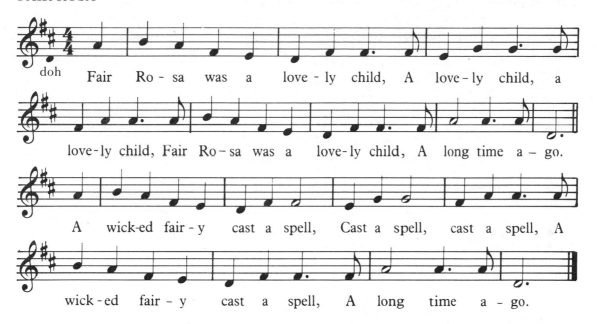

doh | Fair Ro-sa was a love-ly child, A love-ly child, a
love-ly child, Fair Ro-sa was a love-ly child, A long time a-go.
A wick-ed fair-y cast a spell, Cast a spell, cast a spell, A
wick-ed fair-y cast a spell, A long time a-go.

Fair Rosa was a lovely child ,
A lovely child, a lovely child,
Fair Rosa was a lovely child ,
A long time ago .

A wicked fairy cast a spell ,
Cast a spell , cast a spell ,
A wicked fairy cast a spell ,
A long time ago .

Fair Rosa slept for a hundred years ,
A hundred years , a hundred years ,
Fair Rosa slept for a hundred years ,
A long time ago.

The hedges all grew thick and tall ,
Thick and tall , thick and tall ,
The hedges all grew thick and tall ,
A long time ago .

A handsome prince came riding by ,
Riding by , riding by ,
A handsome prince came riding by ,
A long time ago .

He kissed Fair Rosa's lily white hand ,
Lily white hand , lily white hand ,
He kissed Fair Rosa's lily white hand ,
A long time ago.

Fair Rosa will not sleep no more ,
Sleep no more , sleep no more ,
Fair Rosa will not sleep no more ,
A long time ago .

SIR ROGER

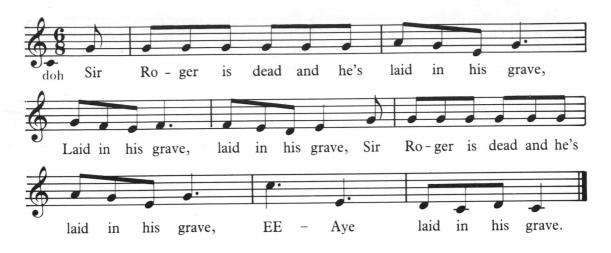

doh Sir Ro - ger is dead and he's laid in his grave,

Laid in his grave, laid in his grave, Sir Ro - ger is dead and he's

laid in his grave, EE - Aye laid in his grave.

Sir Roger is dead and he's laid in his grave ,
Laid in his grave , laid in his grave ,
Sir Roger is dead and he's laid in his grave ,
Ee— aye , laid in his grave .

There grew an old apple tree over his head ,
Over his head , over his head ,
There grew an old apple tree over his head ,
Ee—aye , over his head .

The apples grew ripe and came tumbling down ,
Tumbling down , tumbling down .
The apples grew ripe and came tumbling down ,
Ee—aye , tumbling down .

There came an old woman a-picking them up ,
A-picking them up, a-picking them up ,
There came an old woman a-picking them up ,
Ee—aye , picking them up .

Sir Roger jumped up and he gave her a thump ,
Gave her a thump , gave her a thump ,
Sir Roger jumped up and he gave her a thump ,
Ee—aye , gave her a thump .

Which made the old woman go hippity hop ,
Hippity hop , hippity hop ,
Which made the old woman go hippity hop ,
Ee—aye , hippity hop .

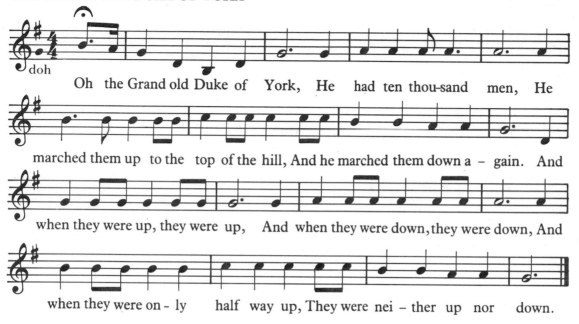

Oh the Grand old Duke of York, He had ten thou-sand men, He marched them up to the top of the hill, And he marched them down a - gain. And when they were up, they were up, And when they were down, they were down, And when they were on - ly half way up, They were nei - ther up nor down.

Oh the Grand old Duke of York ,
He had ten thousand men ,
He marched them up to the top of the hill
And he marched them down again .
And when they were up they were up ,
And when they were down they were down ,
And when they were only half-way up
They were neither up nor down .

As I went a walk-ing one morn-ing in Spring, To hear the birds whist-le__ and the night-in-gales sing, I heard a fair maid-en and sad was her moan: 'Oh, I'm a poor stran-ger and far__ from my home.'

As I went a-walking one morning in spring ,
To hear the birds whistle and the nightingales sing ,
I heard a fair maiden and sad was her moan :
' Oh I'm a poor stranger and far from my home .'

I'll build my love a cottage at the edge of this town
Where the Lords, Dukes and Earls they will not knock it down .
And if the boys ask her why she lives all alone ,
She'll say she's a stranger and far from her home .

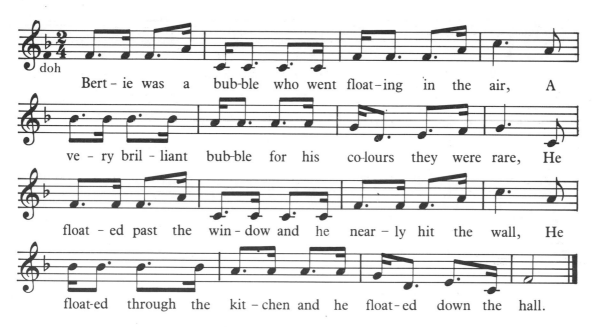

Bert – ie was a bub-ble who went float-ing in the air, A
ve – ry bril – liant bub-ble for his co-lours they were rare, He
float – ed past the win-dow and he near – ly hit the wall, He
float-ed through the kit – chen and he float-ed down the hall.

Bertie was a bubble
who went floating in the air,
A very brilliant bubble
for his colours they were rare.
He floated past the window
and he nearly hit the wall,
He floated through the kitchen
and he floated down the hall,
He was drifting on so nicely,
when a wind blew through the door,
It shook poor Bertie Bubble
and it bounced him on the floor.
Of all the great misfortunes
this surely was the worst,
There was trouble for our bubble,
when poor old Bertie burst.

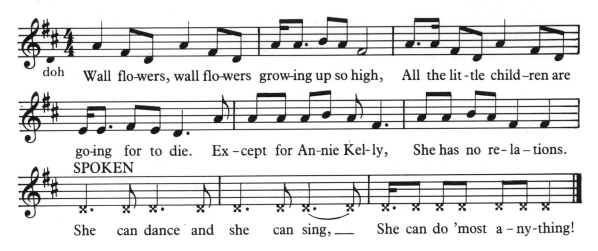

doh Wall flo-wers, wall flo-wers grow-ing up so high, All the lit-tle child-ren are

go-ing for to die. Ex-cept for An-nie Kel-ly, She has no re-la-tions.

SPOKEN

She can dance and she can sing, — She can do 'most a-ny-thing!

Wall flowers , wall flowers ,
Growing up so high ,
All the little children are going for to die .
Except for Annie Kelly ,
She has no relations —
She can dance and she can sing ,
She can do 'most anything !

CHARLIE CHUCK

Charlie Chuck,
Married the duck,
The duck died
And Charlie cried,
Sitting by the fireside.

SICK !

Mammy , Mammy ,
I am sick ,
Send for the doctor ,
Quick , quick , quick .

MRS MASON

Mrs Mason broke a basin ,
Said Mrs Frost ' What did it cost ? '
Mrs O'Dea said ' Fifty P. ',
Said Mrs Hutchison : 'That's too muchison ' .

JESS IN A MESS

Poor old Jess
Got in a mess ,
Spilt her porridge
All over her dress .

FIRE !

Fire , fire , said Mrs Maguire ,
Where , Where , said Mrs O'Hare ,
Down the town , said Mrs Brown ,
Call the brigade , said Mr McGlade .

OVER THE GARDEN WALL

Over the garden wall ,
I let the baby fall ,
My mother came out
And gave me a clout ,
Over the garden wall .

doh

Did you e – ver get a cold in your head, And

have to spend a whole day in bed? Did you e – ver get a snif-fle or a

cough, Or — feel that your nose was fal – ling off? Oh the

snee-zes and the whee-zes and the blows, Did you e-ver get a cold in your nose.

Did you ever get a cold in you head
And have to spend the whole day in bed ?
Did you ever get a sniffle or a cough
Or feel that your nose was falling off ?
O the sneezes and the wheezes and the blows ,
Did you ever get a cold in you nose ?

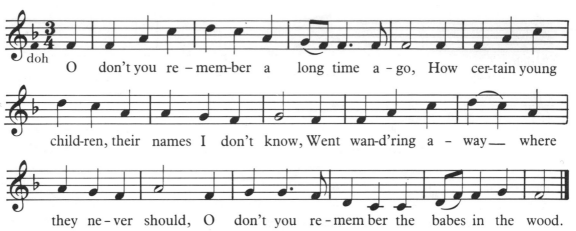

doh

O don't you re – mem-ber a long time a - go, How cer-tain young child-ren, their names I don't know, Went wan-d'ring a - way___ where they ne - ver should, O don't you re - mem ber the babes in the wood.

O don't you remember a long time ago ,
How certain young children their names I don't know ,
Went wandering away where they never should ,
O don't you remember the babes in the wood .

GREEN GRAVEL

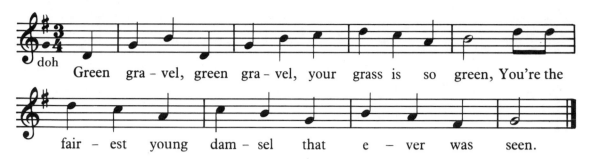

Green gra - vel, green gra - vel, your grass is so green, You're the fair - est young dam - sel that e - ver was seen.

Green Gravel, Green Gravel, your grass is so green,
You're the fairest young damsel that ever was seen.
We washed her, we dried her, we dressed her in silk,
And we wrote down her name with a gold pen and ink.
O Mary, O Mary, your true-love is dead,
And we wrote you a letter to tie round your head.

HOUSE TO LET

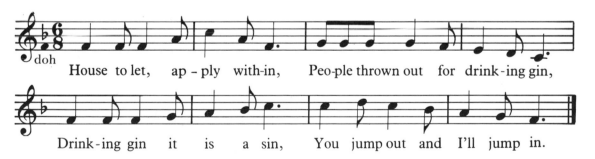

House to let, ap - ply with-in, Peo-ple thrown out for drink-ing gin,
Drink-ing gin it is a sin, You jump out and I'll jump in.

House to let , apply within ,
People thrown out for drinking gin ,
Drinking gin it is a sin ,
You jump out and I'll jump in .

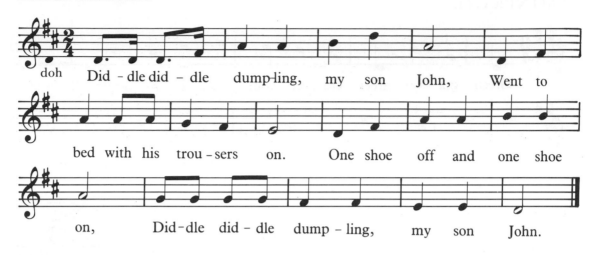

doh Did - dle did – dle dump-ling, my son John, Went to

bed with his trou – sers on. One shoe off and one shoe

on, Did-dle did – dle dump – ling, my son John.

Diddle diddle dumpling , my son John ,
Went to bed with his trousers on .
One shoe off and one shoe on ,
Diddle diddle dumpling , my son John .

doh

La - zy Ma - ry will you get up, Will you get up, will you get up,

La - zy Ma - ry will you get up, On a cold and a frost-y morn - ing.

Lazy Mary will you get up ,
Will you get up , will you get up ,
Lazy Mary will you get up
On a cold and a frosty morning .

No m'dear I won't get up ,
I won't get up, I won't get up ,
No m'dear I won't get up
On a cold and a frosty morning .

If I give you a brush and comb ,
A brush and comb , brush and comb
If I give you a brush and comb ,
On a cold and a frosty morning .

No m'dear etc.

If I give you a watch and chain ,
A watch and chain , a watch and chain ,
If I give you a watch and chain
On a cold and a frosty morning .

No m'dear etc .

If I give a thumpety thump ,
A thumpety thump , a thumpety thump .
If I give you a thumpety thump
On a cold and a frosty morning.

Yes m'dear then I'll get up ,
Then I'll get up , then I'll get up.
Yes m'dear then I'll get up
On a cold and a frosty morning .

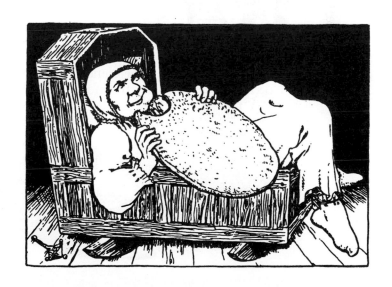

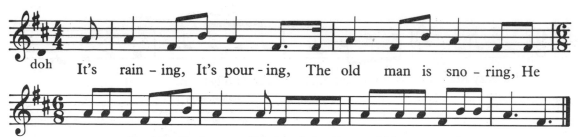

doh It's rain – ing, It's pour – ing, The old man is sno – ring, He

got out of bed And he bumped his head, And he could-'nt get up in the morn-ing.

It's raining ,
It's pouring ,
The old man
Is snoring .
He got out of bed
And he bumped his head ,
And he couldn't get up
In the morning .

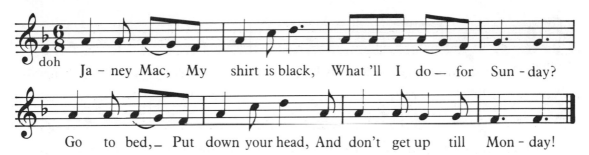

Ja - ney Mac, My shirt is black, What'll I do — for Sun - day?

Go to bed,— Put down your head, And don't get up till Mon - day!

Janey Mac
My shirt is black ,
What'll I do for Sunday ?
Go to bed ,
Put down your head ,
And don't get up till Monday !

ELSIE MARLEY

Elsie Marley is grown so fine
She won't get up to feed the swine ,
But lies in bed till eight or nine ,
Lazy Elsie Marley .

Elsie Marley is so neat
That when she's walking down the street ,
All the boys and girls she'll meet
Say ' There goes Elsie Marley ' .

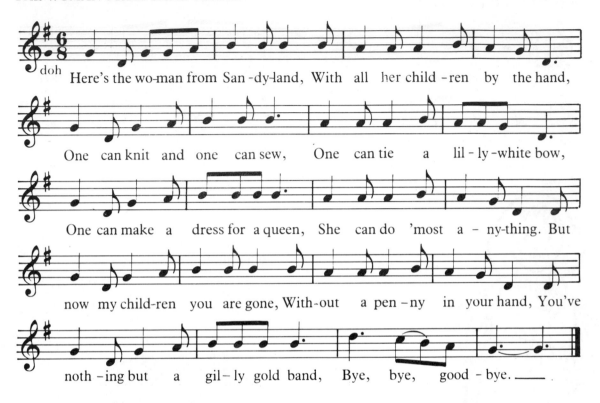

doh Here's the wo-man from San-dy-land, With all her child-ren by the hand,

One can knit and one can sew, One can tie a lil-ly-white bow,

One can make a dress for a queen, She can do 'most a-ny-thing. But

now my child-ren you are gone, With-out a pen-ny in your hand, You've

noth-ing but a gil-ly gold band, Bye, bye, good-bye.

Here's the woman from Sandyland
With all her children by the hand,
One can knit and one can sew,
One can tie a lily-white bow,
One can make a dress for a queen,
She can do 'most anything.
But now my children you are gone
Without a penny in your hand,
You've nothing but a gilly gold band,
Bye, bye, good-bye !

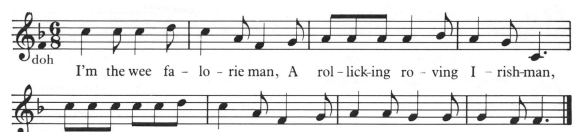

I'm the wee fa – lo – rie man, A rol – lick-ing ro – ving I – rish-man,

I can do a-ny-thing that you can, For I'm the wee Fa – lo – rie man.

I'm the wee Falorie man ,
A rollicking roving Irishman ,
I can do anything that you can
For I'm the wee Falorie man .

TIN CAN DAN

There was an old man
And his name was Dan ,
And he lived at the bottom
Of an old tin can .
He had a pair of slippers
And he turned them into kippers ,
And they all lived together
In the old tin can .

doh Poor old Ro-bin-son Cru – soe, Poor old Ro-bin-son Cru – soe, They made him a coat, Of an old nan-ny goat, I wonder how they could do so. With a ring-a-ding-ding, And a ring-a-ding-ding, Poor old Ro-bin-son Cru – soe.

Poor old Robinson Crusoe ,
Poor old Robinson Crusoe ,
They made him a coat
Of an old nanny goat ,
I wonder how they could do so .
With a ring-a-ding-ding ,
And a ring-a-ding-ding ,
Poor old Robinson Crusoe .

SEEING AND BELIEVING

Did you ever see a purple dog ,
A yellow goose , or a green hog ,
A blue hen , a white fly ?
No you didn't – neither did I .

Did you ever see a yellow dog ,
A grey goose , or a pink hog ,
A brown hen , or a black fly ?
Yes you did , – so did I .

JACKIE MEDORY

I'll tell you a story
Of Jackie Medory ,
And now my story's begun -
I'll tell you another
Of Jackie's young brother
And now my story's done .

Another version :

I'll tell you a story
Of Jackie Medory ,
Shall I begin it ?
That's all that's in it !

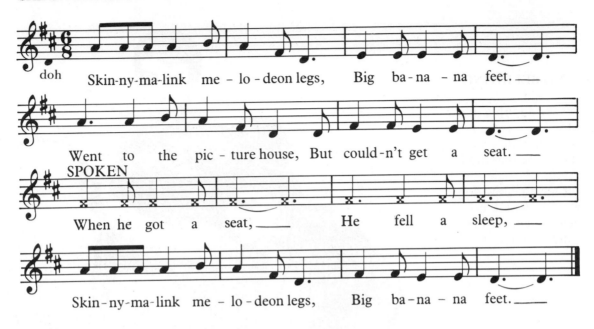

doh Skin-ny-ma-link me-lo-deon legs, Big ba-na-na feet.

Went to the pic-ture house, But could-n't get a seat.

SPOKEN

When he got a seat, He fell a-sleep,

Skin-ny-ma-link me-lo-deon legs, Big ba-na-na feet.

Skinnymalink melodeon legs ,
Big banana feet ,
Went to the picture house
But couldn't get a seat ,
When he got a seat ,
He fell asleep .
Skinnymalink melodeon legs
Big banana feet .

If ever you go to Kilkenny
You'll see a big sign on the wall ,
Saying twenty-four eggs for a penny
And butter for nothing at all .

CURRANTS

Higgledy , Piggledy
Here we lie ,
Picked and plucked
And baked in a pie .
My first is snapping , snarling , growling ,
My second's hard working , romping and prowling .
Higgledy , Piggledy
Here we lie ,
Picked and plucked
And baked in a pie .

THE PRATIES THEY ARE SMALL

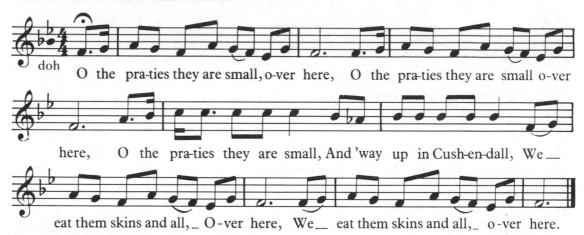

doh

O the pra-ties they are small, o-ver here, O the pra-ties they are small o-ver here, O the pra-ties they are small, And 'way up in Cush-en-dall, We — eat them skins and all, _ O-ver here, We_ eat them skins and all, _ o-ver here.

O the praties they are small over here ,
O the praties they are small over here ,
O the praties they are small ,
And 'way up in Cushendall ,
We eat them skins and all .
Over here .
We eat them skins and all .

AMERICAN TEA

The tea in the US and A ,
Is as weak as dishwater they say ,
It sticks in the spout ,
And it cannot get out ,
The tea in the US and A.

WHISKEY IN MY TAY

It wasn't the man from Garvagh ,
Nor the man from old Kilrea ,
But the dealin' men from Crossmaglen
Put whiskey in my tay .

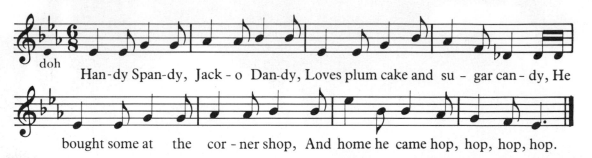

Han-dy Span-dy, Jack - o Dan-dy, Loves plum cake and su - gar can - dy, He

bought some at   the   cor - ner shop, And home he came hop, hop, hop, hop.

Handy Spandy, Jacko Dandy,
Loves plum cake and sugar candy,
He bought some at the corner shop,
And home he came — hop, hop, hop, hop.

HANNAH BANTRY

Han -nah Ban-try, In the pan-try, Gnaw-ing on a mut-ton bone,

She did gnaw it, She did claw it, When she found her-self   a - lone.

Hannah Bantry
In the pantry
Gnawing on a mutton bone,
She did gnaw it,
She did claw it,
When she found herself alone.

doh | My Aunt Jane she asks me in, And she gives me tea out of her wee tin. Half a bap with su- gar on the top, Three black lumps out of her wee shop.

My Aunt Jane she asks me in ,
And gives me tea out of her wee tin .
Half a bap with sugar on the top ,
Three black lumps out of her wee shop .

EAST'S FEAST

Mr East gave a feast ,
Mr North laid the cloth ,
Mr West did his best ,
Mr South burnt his mouth
By eating a cold potato .

IBISTER AND SISTER

Mr Ibister and Bessy his sister
Decided on giving a treat .
So letters they write
Their friends to invite
To their house at the end of the street .

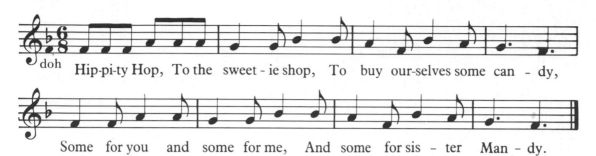

doh | Hip-pi-ty Hop, To the sweet-ie shop, To buy our-selves some can - dy,

Some for you and some for me, And some for sis - ter Man - dy.

Hippity Hop
To the sweetie shop
To buy ourselves some candy ,
Some for you and some for me
And some for sister Mandy .

Hippity Hop
To the sweetie shop
To buy ourselves some candy ,
Some for you and some for me
And some for brother Andy .

PLUMS, ROTTEN AND RIPE

There was an old woman
Who lived in Ardee ,
And in her back garden
She grew a plum tree ,
The plums all grew rotten
Before they grew ripe ,
And the old woman sold them
For tuppence a pint .

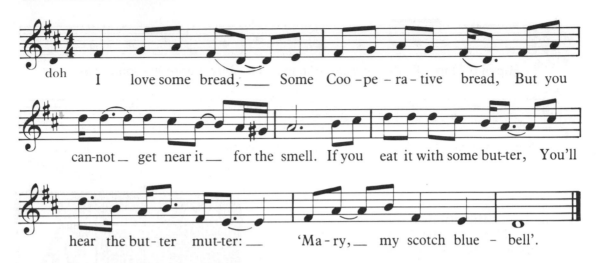

doh | I love some bread, ___ Some Coo-pe-ra-tive bread, But you can-not ___ get near it ___ for the smell. If you eat it with some but-ter, You'll hear the but-ter mut-ter: ___ 'Ma-ry, ___ my scotch blue – bell'.

I love some bread ,
Some Co-operative bread ,
But you cannot get near it for the smell .
If you eat it with some butter ,
You'll hear the butter mutter :
' Mary , my scotch blue bell. '

I love a sausage ,
A Co-operative sausage ,
But you cannot get near it for the smell .
If you eat it with an ingen ,
You'll hear the ingen singing :
' Mary , my scotch blue bell . '

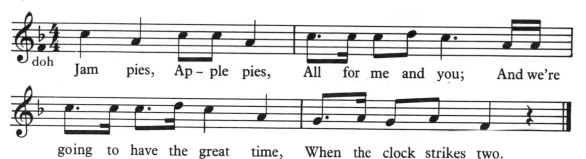

doh | Jam pies, Ap – ple pies, All for me and you; And we're
going to have the great time, When the clock strikes two.

Jam pies , Apples pies
All for me and you ,
And we're going to have the great time
When the clock strikes two .

JELLY AND SAUSAGE

Jelly on the plate ,
Jelly on the plate ,
Wibbely , wobbely ,
Wibbely , wobbely ,
Jelly on the plate .

Sausage in the pan ,
Sausage in the pan ,
Sizzely , sizzely,
Sizzely , sizzely ,
Sausage in the pan .

KILREA FOR DRINKING TAY

Kilrea for drinking tay ,
Garvagh for asses ,
Limavady for Irish lace ,
And Coleraine for lasses .

TWO LITTLE SAUSAGES

doh | Two lit – tle saus – a – ges, Fry – ing in a pan,

One got burnt, And the o – ther said 'SCRAM'

Two little sausages
Frying in the pan ,
One got burnt
And the other said ' scram !

DAVY DUMPLING

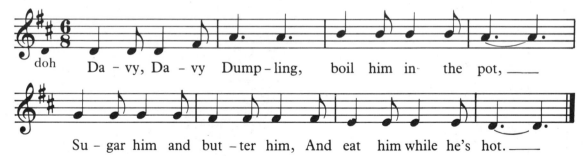

doh | Da – vy, Da – vy Dump – ling, boil him in the pot, ____

Su – gar him and but – ter him, And eat him while he's hot. ____

Davy , Davy , Dumpling ,
Boil him in the pot ,
Sugar him and butter him ,
And eat him while he's hot .

SPUDS

One potato,
Two potato,
Three potato,
Four,
Five potato,
Six potato,
Seven potato,
MORE !

MARY CHERRY

1, 2, 3, 4,
Mary at the cottage door,
5, 6, 7, 8,
Eating cherries off a plate.

FRIENDLY NUMBERS

1 said to 2 :
' How do you do ? '
2 said to 3 :
' As well as you see '
3 said to 4 :
' Step in through the door '
4 said to 5 :
' When did you arrive ? '

KITTENS THAT MEW

1 , 2 , Kittens that mew ,
2 , 3 , Birds in the tree ,
3 , 4 , Shells on the shore ,
4 , 5 , Bees in the hive ,
5 , 6 , The cow that licks .
6 , 7 , Rooks in the heaven .
7 , 8 , Pigs at the gate .
8 , 9 , Clothes on the line .
9 , 10 , A Big Black Hen .

ONE TO FIVE

Number 1 : 'Let's have some fun .'
Number 2 : ' What'll we do ? '
Number 3 : 'We'll have to see. '
Number 4 : 'Tell me more ,'
Number 5 : ' I'm glad I'm alive :

FISH ALIVE

1 , 2 , — 3 , 4 , 5 ,
Once I caught a fish alive .
6 , 7 , — 8 , 9 , 10 ,
Then I put it back again .
Why did you let it go ?
Because it bit my finger so .
Which finger did it bite ?
The little finger on the right .

BUCKLE MY SHOE

1, 2, Buckle my shoe
3, 4, Knock at the door ,
5, 6, Pick up sticks ,
7, 8, Lay them straight ,
9, 10, A big fat hen :

BEE HIVE

1 , 2 —3 , 4 , 5 ,
Bees make honey
In a great big hive .

doh There was an old wo-man tossed up in a bas-ket, Nine-teen times as high as the moon, Where she was go-ing I could-n't but ask it, For in her hand she car-ried a broom. Old wo-man, old wo-man, old wo-man, said I, Where are you go-ing__ up__ so high? To sweep the cob-webs out of the sky.__ May I go with you? Aye, by and by.

There was an old woman tossed up in a basket ,
Nineteen times as high as the moon ,
Where she was going I couldn't but ask it,
For in her hand she carried a broom .
Old woman , old woman, old woman , said I ,
Where are you going up so high ?
To sweep the cobwebs out of the sky .
May I go with you ?
Aye , by and by .

There was a man lived in the moon ,
Lived in the moon , lived in the moon ,
There was a man lived in the moon ,
And his name was Aiken Drum .

He played upon a ladle ,
A ladle , a ladle ,
He played upon a ladle ,
And his name was Aiken Drum .

His hat was made of cream cheese ,
Cream cheese , cream cheese ,
His hat was made of cream cheese ,
And his name was Aiken Drum .

His coat was made of roast beef,
Roast beef , roast beef ,
His coat was made of roast beef ,
And his name was Aiken Drum .

His buttons were made of penny baps ,
Penny baps , penny baps ,
His buttons were made of penny baps ,
And his name was Aiken Drum .

His waistcoat was made of crusty pies ,
Crusty pies , crusty pies ,
His waistcoat was made of crusty pies ,
And his name was Aiken Drum .

His breeks were made of sausage skins ,
Sausage skins , sausage skins ,
His breeks were made of sausage skins
And his name was Aiken Drum .

Another man lived in the moon ,
In the moon , in the moon ,
Another man lived in the moon ,
And his name was Willie Woods .

He ate up all the cream cheese ,
The cream cheese , the cream cheese ,
He ate up all the cream cheese
And his name was Willie Woods.

He ate up all the roast beef ,
The roast beef , the roast beef ,
He ate up all the roast beef ,
And his name was Willie Woods .

He ate up all the penny baps ,
The penny baps , the penny baps ,
He ate up all the penny baps ,
And his name was Willie Woods .

He ate up all the crusty pies ,
The crusty pies , the crusty pies ,
He ate up all the crusty pies ,
And his name was Willie Woods .

But he choked upon the sausage skins ,
The sausage skins , the sausage skins ,
He choked upon the sausage skins ,
And that ended Willie Woods.

THE MAN IN THE MOON

The man in the moon
Looked out of the moon ,
Looked out of the moon and said :
' It's time for all children
That live down below
To think about going to bed .'

WISHING STAR

Starlight star bright ,
First star I see tonight ,
I wish I may ,
I wish I might ,
Have the wish
I wish tonight .

MOON PENNY

Moon penny as bright as silver ,
Come and play with little childer.

NEWS OF THE DAY

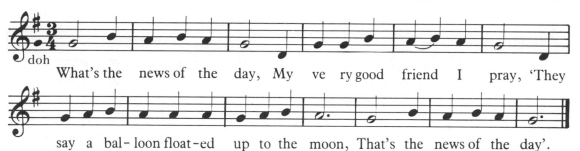

What's the news of the day, My ve ry good friend I pray, 'They say a bal- loon float-ed up to the moon, That's the news of the day'.

What's the news of the day
My very good friend I pray ,
They say a balloon floated up to the moon ,
That's the news of the day .

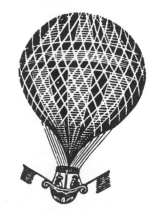

ON SATURDAY NIGHT

On Sa-tur-day night, I lost my wife, And didn't know where to find her, She was up in the moon, Play-ing a tune, And all of the stars a – round her.

On saturday night
I lost my wife
And didn't know here to find her
She was up in the moon .
Playing a tune
And all of the stars around her.

SALLY GO ROUND THE MOON

doh Sal – ly go round the moon, _____ Sal – ly go round the

stars, _____ Sal – ly go round the chim – ney pots, WHOOPS!

Sally go round the moon ,
Sally go round the stars ,
Sally go round the chimney pots ,
WHOOPS !
Sally go round the moon ,
Sally go round the stars ,
Every Sunday after mass ,
WHOOPS !

I SEE THE MOON

doh I see the moon, And the moon sees me, God bless the moon, And God bless me.

I see the moon ,
And the moon sees me ,
God bless the moon
And God bless me .

THREE SAINTS

In Down three saints one grave do fill ,
Bridget , Patrick , and Columbkille .

MUNSTER FOR LEARNING

Munster for learning ,
Leinster for the beef ,
Connacht for the beggerman ,
And Ulster for the thief .

St Patrick was a gentleman,
He came of decent people ,
In Dublin town he built a church
And put on it a steeple.
His father was a Brallaghan ,
His mother was a Brady ,
His Auntie an O'Callaghan ,
His uncle an O'Grady ,
So success to bold St Patrick's fist,
He was a saint so clever ,
He gave the snakes an awful twist
And banished them forever .

ESAU

I saw Esau
Sitting on a see-saw ,
Esau he saw me .
I saw Esau
Sitting on a see-saw —
Esau , 1 , 2 , 3 ,

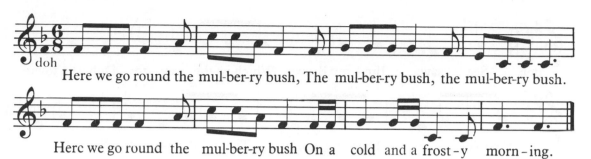

Here we go round the mul-ber-ry bush, The mul-ber-ry bush, the mul-ber-ry bush.

Here we go round the mul-ber-ry bush On a cold and a frost-y morn-ing.

Here we go round the mulberry bush,
The mulberry bush , the mulberry bush ,
Here we go round the mulberry bush,
On a cold and a frosty morning .

This is the way we get out of bed ,
Get out of bed , get out of bed ,
This is the way we get out of bed ,
On a cold and a frosty morning .

This is the way we boil the eggs ,
Boil the eggs , boil the eggs ,
This is the way we boil the eggs ,
On a cold and a frosty morning .

This is the way we go to school ,
Go to school , go to school .
This is the way we go to school ,
On a cold and a frosty morning .

This is the way we run out to play ,
Run out to play , run out to play ,
This is the way we run out to play ,
On a cold and a frosty morning .

JIMMY BROWN

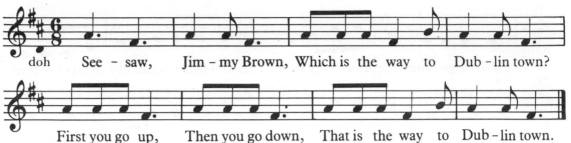

doh See - saw, Jim - my Brown, Which is the way to Dub - lin town?

First you go up, Then you go down, That is the way to Dub - lin town.

See-saw , Jimmy Brown ,
Which is the way to Dublin town ?
First you go up ,
Then you go down ,
That is the way to Dublin town .

STORMY WEATHER

doh Storm-y weath-er, Wind-y weath-er, When the wind blows, We'll all go to-gether.

Stormy weather ,
Windy weather ,
When the wind blows
We'll all go together .

doh Je – re – mi – ah, Blow the fire, ___ Puff, puff, puff,

First you blow it gent - i – ly, And then you blow it rough.

Jeremiah
Blow the fire
Puff puff puff.
First you blow it gent-i-ly,
And then you blow it rough.

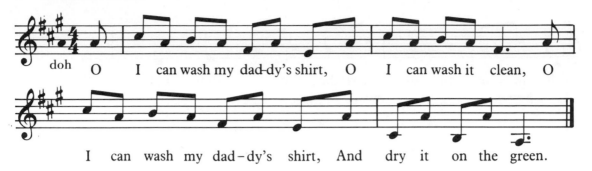

doh   O   O I can wash my dad-dy's shirt,   O   I   can wash it   clean,   O

I   can wash my dad-dy's shirt, And   dry   it   on the green.

O I can wash my daddy's shirt ,
   O I can wash it clean ,
O I can wash my daddy's shirt
   And dry it on the green .

SHADOWS

I see a shadow on the wall ,
I see it rise , I see it fall .
Whose shadow is it that I see ?
I think I know , I think it's me .

I see a shadow on the wall ,
I see it rise , I see it fall .
Whose shadow is it , wish I knew ,
I think I do , I think it's you .

HELPING OUT

When I was a little boy
I washed my mammy's dishes ,
I stuck my finger in the pud
And said it was delicious .

NIGHT NIGHT

Night night ,
Sleep tight ,
Dont let the bugs bite .
If they bite ,
Squeeze them tight ,
And they won't bite
Another night .

Explanatory notes on some of the rhymes and songs :

The old pig (p 33), *Muc :* pig in the Irish language.
An madairin Rua (p 36) translation :
 The little red dog (fox), red, red, red, red, red,
 The little red dog is ugly,
 The little red dog is lying in the rushes
 With his two ears cocked on high.
The shepherd's lamb (p 47) translation of chorus :
 And O, I hail, I hail you,
 You are the love of my heart without deceit
 And O , I hail, I hail you,
 You are the little pet of your mother.
Snail song (p 48) *Seilide Seilide Pucai*
 phonetically : shelli deh pookey.
Binn Beagles (p 48) *brocks :* from the Irish broc (badger)
Play pins : Christmas game (p 73)
 One player conceals a pin in the hand, the other
 player points at both hands in turn following the
 rhythm of the words and wins if the last word
 coincides with pointing at the hand holding the pin.
My Aunt Jane (p 121) *bap :* Ulster expression for bun.

Apart from the original illustrations mentioned on the
acknowledgement page, all other pictures hail from a
variety of chapbooks, balladsheets and nurseryrhyme
books such as :

 Andrew Lang's 'Nursery Rhyme Book ' of 1898
illustrated by L.Leslie Brooke, from ' Sing Song' of 1872
illustrated by Arthur Hughes and Edward Lear's
'Nonsense Songs and Stories ' illustrated by himself(1871)

Bill Meek was born in 1937 and grew up in a small community on the shores of Strangford Lough in County Down. Throughout his life he has been involved with all manner of traditional music and song as a performer, broadcaster, collector and writer. A special interest in the rhymes, songs and street games of childhood led to his presenting the RTE pre-school series ' Singawhile '. He now works as a radio producer and lives in Dublin.

Ossian Publications publish a large range of music books relating to many aspects of Irish Music. For a complete and up-to-date list of music published and distributed , send your name and adress with an international reply coupon (printed matter stamp in Ireland) to :

OSSIAN PUBLICATIONS

Publishers and Distributors of Irish & General Printed Music

21 Iona Green, Cork, Ireland